The Great Dolphin Rescue

by Myka-Lynne Sokoloff
illustrated by Nicole Wong

Harcourt
SCHOOL PUBLISHERS

Requests for permission to make copies of any part of the work should be addressed to School Permissions and Copyrights, Harcourt, Inc., 6277 Sea Harbor Drive, Orlando, Florida 32887–6777. Fax: 407-345-2418.

HARCOURT and the Harcourt Logo are trademarks of Harcourt, Inc., registered in the United States of America and/or other jurisdictions.

Printed in China

ISBN 10: 0-15-350277-0
ISBN 13: 978-0-15-350277-4

Ordering Options
ISBN 10: 0-15-349940-0 (Grade 5 ELL Collection)
ISBN 13: 978-0-15-349940-1 (Grade 5 ELL Collection)
ISBN 10: 0-15-357312-0 (package of 5)
ISBN 13: 978-0-15-357312-5 (package of 5)

3 4 5 6 7 8 9 10   468   12 11 10 09 08

My older brother, José, had just won his fourth swim race. He was a very good swimmer. He was the champion of our swim team. I wasn't very good at swimming.

"You'll find something you are good at," Mama said. I didn't believe her, though.

One day, Tara stopped by. She is my best friend. She doesn't care about swim races. "Wow, you look really sad," she said. Don't you love people who tell the truth?

Tara invited me to Sea Circus. It's a fun place where you can see different sea animals do tricks in a big pool. I had never seen sea lions or dolphins before. I wanted to see the animals. However, I didn't want to think about pools or swimming. Just the thought of water made me upset.

I decided I loved dolphins too much to miss the
Sea Circus. I was just feeling grumpy. I would feel
better later.

Tara's dad took us. We drove on the highway with
the windows open. The sun and fresh air felt good.

We showed our tickets at the gate. A woman
took us to our seats. We were right in the front row.
I imagined the dolphins splashing us. Many people
filled the seats around us. I would never perform for
an audience with that many people!

The show began. Soon I forgot about everything else. The animals did amazing tricks in a huge pool. Sea lions balanced balls and other toys on their noses. Two dolphins jumped through hoops. The dolphins worked together as a team. Then the dolphins took a fish from the trainer's mouth.

I noticed something odd in the middle of the show. One dolphin had a long scar. At first, I could not take my eyes off the animal.

The animal was very graceful in the water. The dolphin swam like a great dancer dances. I could tell the dolphin was very smart. It looked so happy. I think it loved doing each trick and getting a fish as a reward. One time, the dolphin splashed us. He was playing. I think he did it on purpose to show that he liked us!

I forgot about swim races. I watched the dolphins. "Thank you for taking me, Tara. That was really fun," I said as we left Sea Circus.

A few weeks later, my family and I went to the beach for a vacation. I was excited about going. I had never seen the ocean before.

When we got there, everyone was talking about José's latest win. I knew if I stayed inside our rented beach house, I would be safe from the conversation. However, I felt lonely and bored.

One day, I finally got tired of staying indoors. I decided to take a walk on the beach. I wore my big, dark glasses and large, floppy hat. The day was beautiful. Maybe nobody would notice me.

I saw something unusual that day when I got to the beach. I will never forget it. A large dolphin was lying on the sand near the edge of the sea. The animal made soft noises and looked sad.

It must have just washed up on the beach. People ran to the dolphin. "It needs to stay wet," a woman yelled. "Get some towels, Marta," Mama said. I ran and grabbed some beach towels. I put them in the water. Then we covered the dolphin. The towels kept it cool in the hot sun.

A man said, "Sometimes dolphins swim to the beach when the tide is high. Then they can get stuck when the water level goes down. Nobody knows why they come so close to shore."

A large crowd gathered on the beach. Some people thought we should try to push the dolphin back in the water. I went to help.

We all pushed gently at first. We did not want to hurt the beautiful creature. The dolphin did not move. It took long, deep breaths. The poor thing was shaking with fear. The dolphin looked me in the eye. "Please save me," the dolphin seemed to say.

We pushed harder. As I worked, my glasses and hat fell off. I didn't pick them up. I was too busy. I wanted to save the dolphin.

As I helped, I did not have any worries about swimming. I did not mind the cold water. I did not mind being close to all those people. I just felt full of hope. It felt good to work with other people. I did not think about myself for the whole time.

Suddenly, I remembered the dolphin with the scar at Sea Circus. The dolphin was beautiful. I loved watching it swim, jump, and do tricks. That dolphin taught me a lesson: *You don't have to be perfect. Forget about yourself. Do something for others.* Now I returned the favor.

We all gave one big, final push. Then our dolphin swam off into the sea! I know it turned back and looked me in the eye. I think it was saying thank you.

A little boy was watching from the beach. When I got near, he asked, "What happened to that dolphin?"

"It was stranded on the beach," I answered. "Some other people and I helped it back into the water."

"Will the dolphin live?" he asked.

I felt fearless at that moment. I had helped save a beautiful creature that needed me to live. I looked the boy in the eye. "The dolphin is safe now," I told the boy. "We were all pulling for it. I think it knew that." Somehow, I thought, the dolphin was pulling for me, too.

Scaffolded Language Development

USING CONTRACTIONS Remind students that contractions are made up of two words that are combined and shortened by leaving a letter or letters out. An apostrophe takes the place of the missing letter or letters. Write the following examples on the board and model crossing out the letters and replacing them with an apostrophe to make the contraction:

is not/isn't   have not/can't   did not/didn't   will not/won't

For further practice, have students turn the following sentences into negative statements using a contraction.

1. It is time for the dolphins to eat.
2. I can hold my breath for a long time.
3. He does know how to swim very well.
4. We will get to the beach before lunch.

 Social Studies

Locate Dolphins Help students look up where dolphins live in the world. Make a list of the locations and have students find them on a map or globe. Then have students write some sentences about where dolphins live.

School-Home Connection

Family Cooperation Have students discuss with family members ways they might work together when a family member's feelings get hurt.

Word Count: 954